Introduction to the iPad and iPhone

I0004866

Getting Organised with The Calendar App

© 2017 iTandCoffee

iOS 11 Edition

Special Sales and Supply Queries

For any information about buying this title in bulk quantities, or for supply of this title for educational or fund-raising purposes, contact iTandCoffee on **1300 885 420** or email **enquiry@itandcoffee.com.au**.

iTandCoffee classes and private appointments

For queries about classes and private appointments with iTandCoffee, call **1300 885 420** or email **enquiry@itandcoffee.com.au**.

iTandCoffee operates in and around Glen Iris, Victoria in Australia.

Introducing iTandCoffee ...

iTandCoffee is a Melbourne-based business that was founded in 2012, by IT professional Lynette Coulston.

Lynette and the staff at iTandCoffee have a passion for helping others - especially women of all ages - to enter and navigate the new, and often daunting, world of technology.

At iTandCoffee, **patience is our virtue.**

You'll find a welcoming smile, a relaxed cup of tea or coffee, and a genuine enthusiasm for helping you to gain the confidence to use and enjoy your technology.

With personalised appointments and small, friendly classes – either at our bright, comfortable, cafe-style shop in Glen Iris or at your place - we offer a brand of technology support and education that is so hard to find.

At iTandCoffee, you won't find young 'techies' who speak in a foreign language and move at a pace that leaves you floundering and 'bamboozled'!

Our focus is on helping you to use your technology in a way that enhances your personal and/or professional life – to feel more informed, organised, connected and entertained!

4

iTandCoffee
Relax, we'll help you get iT

Call on iTandCoffee for help with all sorts of technology – Apple, Windows, iCloud, Evernote, Dropbox, all sorts of other Apps (including Microsoft Office products), getting you set up on the internet, setting up a printer, and so much more.

Here are just some of the topics covered in our regular classes at iTandCoffee:

- Introduction to the iPad and iPhone
- The next step on your iPad and iPhone
- Bring your Busy Life under Control using the iPad and iPhone
- Getting to know your Mac
- Understanding and using iCloud
- An Organised Life with Evernote
- Taking and Managing photos on the iPhone and iPad
- Travel with your iPad, iPhone and other technology.
- Keeping kids safe on the iPad, iPhone and iPod Touch.
- Staying Safe Online

The iTandCoffee website (itandcoffee.com.au) offers a wide variety of resources for those brave enough to venture online to learn more: handy hints for iPad, iPhone and Mac; videos and slideshows of iTandCoffee classes; guides on a range of topics; a blog covering all sorts of topical events.

We also produce a regular Handy Hint newsletter full of information that is of interest to our clients and subscribers.

Hopefully, that gives you a bit of a picture of iTandCoffee and what we are about. Please don't hesitate to iTandCoffee on 1300 885 420 to discuss our services or to make a booking.

We hope you enjoy this guide, and find its contents informative and useful. Please feel free to offer feedback at feedback@itandcoffee.com.au.

Regards,

Lynette Coulston (iTandCoffee Owner)

Getting Organised with The Calendar App

TABLE OF CONTENTS

Getting Organised with The Calendar App

TABLE OF CONTENTS

Introduction

The Calendar App allows you to replace or complement your current diary and wall calendar, providing a great way of tracking yours, and your family's events and appointments - and providing you with many features that your old diary and calendar can't match.

Try to use your iPad/iPhone Calendar as much as possible to record everything that's coming up.

You may find that, over time, you no longer need your 'manual' calendars. Especially for those of you that have an iPhone, this will mean that your calendar is with you wherever you go.

Depending on your settings and the number of mail accounts that you have installed on your iPad or iPhone, the calendars you see in your Calendar App may be from one or more mail accounts.

Your iCloud, Gmail, Exchange, Yahoo, Outlook and other mail accounts can all have calendars associated with them.

The calendars that your Calendar app uses are defined in **Settings -> Accounts & Passwords**. Tap on each of your **Accounts** to see if the **Calendars** setting is turned on. (Below shows my Gmail account settings.)

If **Calendars** is on, then this mail account's calendar will be able to be viewed in the **Calendar** app.

Many of the features of the **Calendar** app that are described by this guide apply to all account calendars.

However, others are special features that will apply only to calendars from your iCloud account.

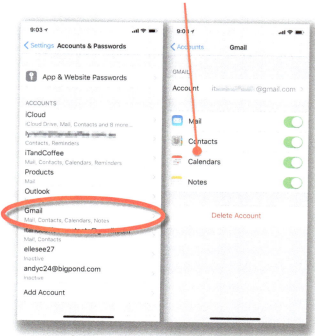

Why use the Calendar app?

You can use the Calendar App to record:

- Appointments
- Meetings
- Kids' sporting events
- Dinners and social engagements
- Birthdays and anniversaries
- Lots more!

Why is an iPad/iPhone Calendar better than an old fashioned one diary or wall calendar?

It can be with you on the go and, if you sync using iCloud, it is available on your iPad/iPhone and computer.

Unlike your written calendar, your iPad/iPhone calendar can remind you of an upcoming event with an alert. You can even ask it to remind you twice. It can even tell you when it's time to leave based on current traffic conditions.

Your Calendar allows you to easily record regular events, such as swimming lessons or your pilates class – enter once and your repeating event will appear as many times as you ask it to.

You can also colour-code your calendar by creating more than one 'calendar' – e.g. one for home, one for work, one that you want to share with your husband, and one that you don't!

I can guarantee it will always look much tidier than your diary or wall calendar. Here are some other great features of your Calendar

- You can invite others to your calendar event – for example, when organizing a girls' night out.
- There is even room for notes and information about the event's location and any other details you might need to remember.
- Sometimes, you can quickly add an event to your calendar with date/time information from an email or web page.
- You can ask Siri to schedule your events for you.

Different ways of viewing your calendar

Your viewing options

On the iPad, your options for viewing your calendar are shown along the top of the screen on the iPad.

On your iPhone, your different views are little less obvious.

Day View on the iPad

On your iPad, the options available for viewing your calendar are 'Day', Week, Month, and 'Year'.

Let's look first at the **Day** view on the iPad. Touch on **Day** at the top of the screen to view your day's events or to add new events.

The **Day** view shows your calendar of events for the date that is currently selected along the top – in the below example, Wed 6th January 2016 is selected.

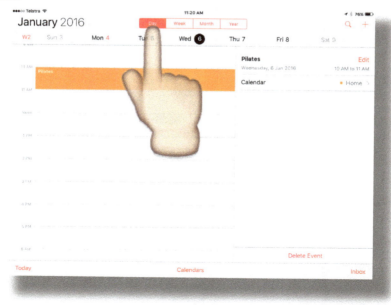

Different ways of viewing your calendar

It is like looking at a page of a diary that shows just one day at a time.

To view a different day in the same week, touch on a different date along the top.

To move to a different week, drag or swipe your finger across the bar of dates to see the next week – use a 'swipe and flick' gesture to move the bar quickly to the next week.

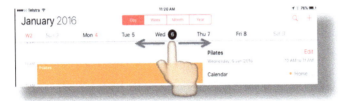

To view the details of one of the events shown on your calendar, just tap on it.

The right-hand side of your **Day** view will show whatever information is recorded about that event. In the below example, the 'orange' event is selected and therefore shown on the right.

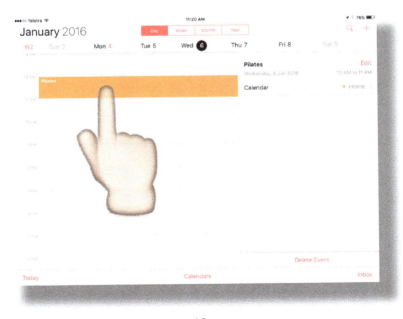

Different ways of viewing your calendar

Use your finger on the left-hand side to drag your day's timeslots up and down – this is helpful if you wish to see appointments earlier and/or later in the day.

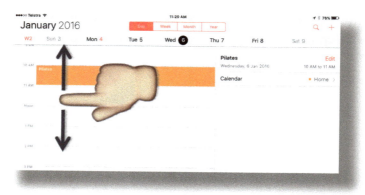

Day view on your iPhone

On your iPhone, there is no **Day** word to tap to see your **Day** view.

You must touch on the date you require, either from your **Year** view of the calendar (below left) or from your **Month** view (below middle). This will give you the **Day** view (far right below).

Once in your **Day** view, the same principles apply as for your iPad for changing the date that you are viewing – i.e. touch or swipe the dates at the top to move to a different date (as shown below right).

Different ways of viewing your calendar

Getting to 'Today' quickly!

On both the iPad and the iPhone, if you want to find the current date quickly, just tap on **Today**, which is shown at the bottom left on the iPad and iPhone.

Week View on the iPad

On your iPad, you can see a full week in one glance by choosing the **Week** option at the top. Touch on any event to see details pop up next to it.

All-day events show at top.

Once again, swipe the 'date' bar at the top of the screen left and right to move between dates and weeks.

Select **Today** (bottom left) to go straight to today's date in **Week** view.

Tap on any event in this view to view further details about that event.

Different ways of viewing your calendar

Week View on the iPhone

On your iPhone, it is not so obvious how to get to your **Week** view!

You'll need to hold your phone on its side!

Whenever your phone is on this angle, your Calendar App will show the **Week** view.

Swipe up and down to view the day's events, and left to right to move from day to day and week to week.

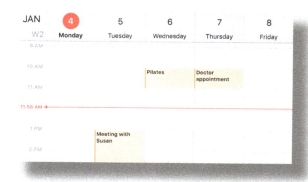

Note. If you have a 'Plus' model of the iPhone, you will find that in 'landscape' orientation, you have similar Day, Week, Month, Year options to those visible on the iPad.)

Different ways of viewing your calendar

Month View on the iPad

On your iPad, the **Month** view looks the most like your wall calendar. From your iPad, you could take screen photo of it, print it and put it on your wall!

To move between the months, **swipe up and down**.

Month View on the iPhone

On your iPhone, how you get your **Month** view depends on the view that you are currently seeing. If you are seeing your **Day** view (below), touch on the month that is shown at the top left of the screen to see your Month view for that month.

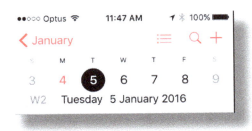

Different ways of viewing your calendar

If you are currently in your **Year** view (see below left), touch on any day in the month to view the **Month** view for that month.

When viewing your **Month** view (see below), a grey dot on any date shows you have one or more events on that date.

Today's date is highlighted in red.

Move between months in your **Month** view by dragging or swiping up and down.

On your iPhone, touch on any day in the month to see the **Day** view of that date.

Daily Events in Month View

On your iPhone, Touch on the 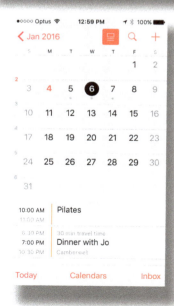 symbol at the top of the Month view to enter a mode that allows you to view events while in this Month view.

When the symbol at the top is highlighted in red, you can touch on any day in your month view and view a list of the day's events in the bottom section of the screen.

Drag your finger up and down in either of the sections of the screen to see more – in the top section to see other months, in the bottom section to see events for the day that are not in view.

Different ways of viewing your calendar

Year View on the iPad

On your iPad, you can view a full year by selecting the 'Year' view.

A shaded red circle highlights today's date.

Drag of flick up and down to move through the years in Year view.

Tap on any day in any month to go to that month's **Month** view.

Year View on the iPhone

On your iPhone, you can access your **Year** view when you are looking at a Month view.

Just tap on the <Year at the top left to see your phone's **Year** view.

As shown far right, this shows your year's calendar.

Drag up and down to view previous and future years.

Today's date (if in view) will be circled in red.

Return to a particular month by touching on any date in that month.

18

Adding an event – the basics first

There are a few of different ways to add events to your calendar – we'll cover the first three here.

Add a new event using '+'

1. Just tap the +

With the Calendar app open in any of the calendar views, you can tap the Add (+) option at the top right to create an event.

2. Give your event a title

As a minimum, you'll have to provide a **Title** for the event.

3. Define the start and end time

If the event is to last 'all day, turn on the **All-Day** switch.

Otherwise, define the Start and End Times.

Tap on the **Starts** field – this will give you some 'scrollers' for selecting the date and time of the event (see image below).

Drag your finger up and down over the date shown to see the dates change – the one that is not greyed is the one that you have selected.

Then do the same for the hour, then minutes and 'am/pm'.

By default, your event duration will be set for 1 hour. To modify the end time, touch on the **Ends** field. Follow the same process as for **Starts** to select the date and time.

4. Now you are done!

This is enough to create your event – press **Add** to add the event to your calendar. Alternatively, if you have decided not to go ahead with adding the event, simply tap **Cancel**.

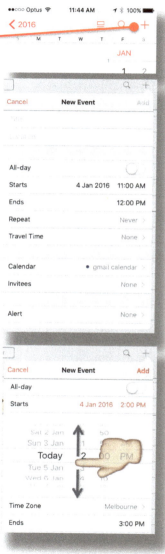

Adding an event – the basics first

Add a new event using 'touch and hold' method

This is the method I love using to create events in my Calendar.

While in a 'Day' or Week view, hold your finger on the calendar at the time you want to schedule the event until you see a 'New Event' pop up, then let go.

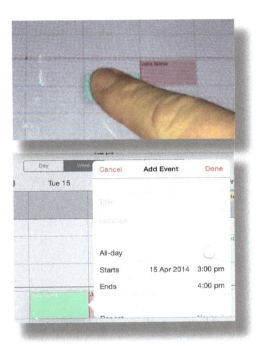

1. Give your event a title

Your new event has been created, and now all you need to do is **name it** – the start and end times are already filled in!

2. Now you are done!

After you have named your event, press **Done** (top right) to finish.

This can be a real time saver.

If you leave your finger on a new event after it has appeared (don't lift it), you will be able to move the event around to ensure it starts at the required time.

Ask Siri to add your event

If you are brave enough to use Siri – your inbuilt personal assistant on your iPad and iPhone, scheduling an event can be as simple as asking Siri to do it for you.

Simply use words that Siri 'understands'. Here are some examples:

- Add doctor's appointment at 10am tomorrow
- Schedule Pilates every Monday at 9am
- Set up a meeting with Charlie at 9
- Set up a meeting about Christmas party tomorrow at 9am.

Adding a Location to your event

You'll notice when you create an event that there is a **Location** field below the **Title**.

Record the address or location for your event in this field – preferably a location that is recognised by Maps.

As you start typing the event location, suggested Recent locations, Contact addresses and Map locations will appear below.

If you see the required location, tap it to add it to the Location field.

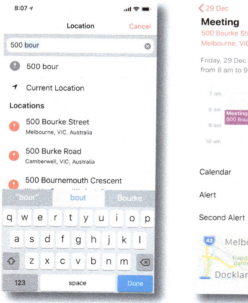
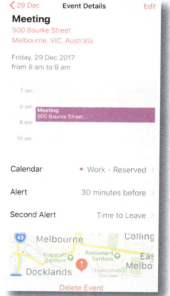

Adding a recognised Maps location to your event has several benefits:

• Your event will show a Map with the location of the event. Tap on this map to go to the Maps app and, if desired, request directions.

• Your Calendar app can then provide an automatic **Time to Leave alert** that is addition to the 'default' alert that you set up for your events. (We cover how to enable these default alerts a bit later.)

Changing an event

Once an event has been created, you can change its details – to change the name, location, time, duration, add a reminder, add a note and much more.

There are a couple of ways to do this, depending on what it is you want to change.

To change various details about your event

1. Tap on the event from any calendar view.

2. A preview of the event will appear (see below).

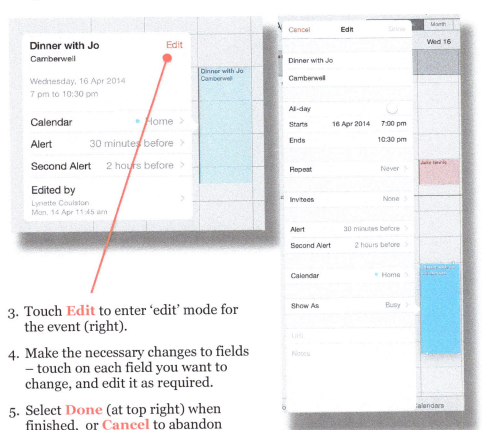

3. Touch **Edit** to enter 'edit' mode for the event (right).

4. Make the necessary changes to fields – touch on each field you want to change, and edit it as required.

5. Select **Done** (at top right) when finished, or **Cancel** to abandon changes.

Changing an event

Change the start time or end time using the 'touch and move' or 'touch and drag' method.

You can change the start and end time, or even the date of an event, directly on the calendar when you are looking at the **Day** or **Week** view – without having to go into **Edit** mode for the event.

1. Touch and hold on the event for a second or so.

2. You will see the event turn 'bold' and two dots appear – one at the top, and one at the bottom.

3. Hold your finger on the top dot and move your finger upwards or downwards to make the start time earlier or later.

4. Hold your finger on the bottom dot and move your finger upwards or downwards to make the end time earlier or later.

5. Changes can be made in 15 minute intervals – look over on the left side to see of the time that you currently have selected as you are moving the event.

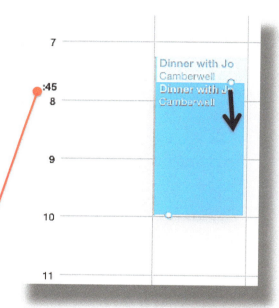

6. When the event is bolded and has the two dots, you can touch and move the entire event – to an earlier or later time, or to an entirely different day. Just touch in the middle, then drag to move it to its new date and time. Simple!

Changing an event

Move an event to a different day with touch and drag

When you are looking at your calendar in the **Month** view on your iPad, you can move events to a different day in that month view.

1. Touch and hold on the event until you see it surrounded by a colour (the colour will be determined by your choice of calendar for the event – we'll look at this later).

2. Without lifting your finger, move the event to a different date – this date can be on a different 'page'.

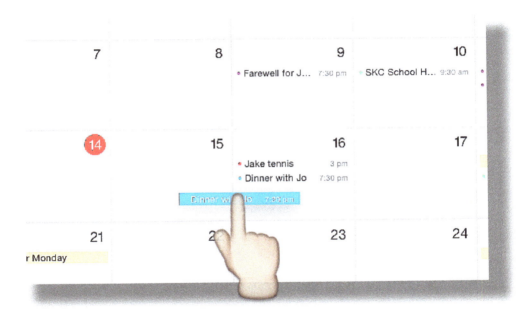

3. Let go when you are positioned on the new date.

4. Your event will have the same start and end time as previously, just on a different date.

Experiment with this one. You can move the event to a different week when in **Week** view by going to the right or left edge of the calendar; or move to a different month in **Month** view by moving to the top or bottom edge.

Deleting an event

Deleting an event that is no longer required is as simple as touching on the event in your calendar and selecting "**Delete Event**" at the bottom, and confirming your action:

It is also possible to delete an event while in **Edit** mode.

1. Touch on the event in the calendar

2. Touch **Edit** (top right) to view the event in 'Edit' mode.

3. Drag up to scroll to bottom of the 'Edit' screen.

4. Select **Delete Event**.

5. A confirmation screen will appear.

6. Touch **Delete Event** to confirm, or **Cancel** if you change your mind.

Calendar reminders

Set a reminder for an individual event

When creating an event, you can choose if you want to receive a reminder alert prior to the event, in the form of a sound and a reminder message that pops up on the screen.

You can set a customized alert for each event that you create – at the time that you create the event, or later by **Edit**ing the event.

When you are creating the event or viewing it in **Edit** mode:

1. Touch on the **Alert** field – you may need to drag up to see this field.

2. Choose when you would like to be alerted (see sample screen below) - the options you can see will depend on whether or not the event is a 'full day' event.

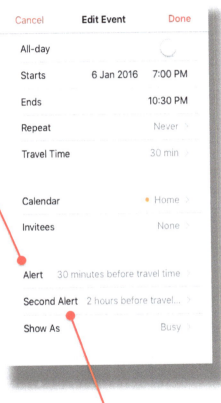

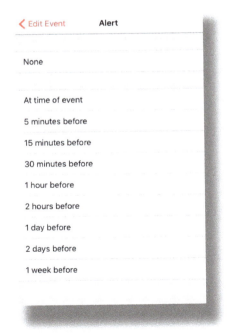

3. If you would like to set up a second alert, touch on the **Second Alert** field and choose when to be alerted.

Calendar Reminders

Set up standard alerts

You can set up standard alert times (e.g. 30 minutes before, one day before) for different 'types' of calendar event. It is a good idea to do this, so that you don't have to remember to choose an Alert timeframe every time you create an event.

1. Go to **Settings**, then to **Calendar**.

2. Look for **Default Alert Times**.

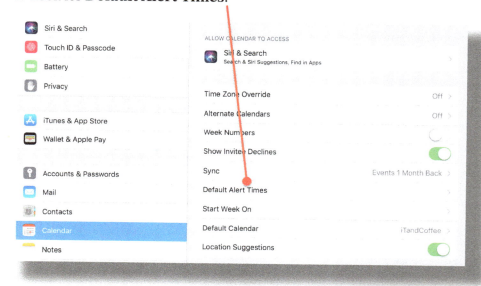

3. Define default alerts for each type of event: **Event**, **All-Day Events** and for **Birthdays** (more later). Simply tap on each of these and choose the required alert time.

4. You will also notice an extra option here called **Time to Leave**. If you would like to receive an

automatically generated alert that is based on the location of your event (if specified) and the current traffic – and determed based on the time it would take to get to the event's location - turn this option On.

Calendar Reminders

Choosing how your Calendar 'Alerts' are notified

You can choose what form your Calendar event alerts should take – whether they should pop up as 'Alerts' in the middle of the screen or whether they should be messages that appear briefly at the top of the screen (called 'Banners').

You can also specify whether you want your calendar reminder notifications to appear in your Notification Centre – the area that appears when you swipe down from the top of the screen.

The whole area of Notifications is covered separately in the iTandCoffee guide **A Guided Tour of the iPad and iPhone**, but for those brave enough to explore this area now...

1. Go to **Settings->Notifications.**

2. Select the 'Calendar' app from the list on the right-hand side.

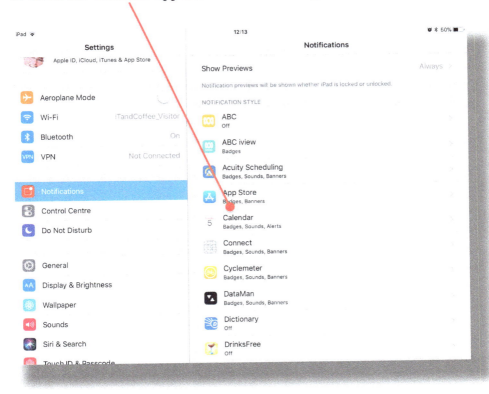

Calendar Reminders

3. Tap on **Upcoming Events** to bring up the menu so you can choose the type of notification that should apply.

4. Choose where and how you wish your **Upcoming Event** notifications to be seen.

5. You can also choose the sound that is made by the calendar event reminder.

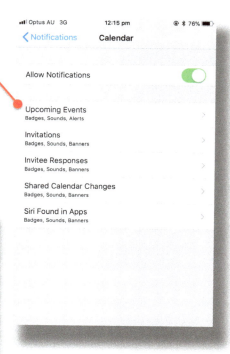

You will see there ar other types of notification that apply for the Calendar app.

Choose the notification style for each of these (or leave them set as the default).

Creating Repeating Events

You will often need to schedule events that occur on a regular basis – for example, a weekly pilates class. Such events are known as 'recurring' or 'repeating' events.

1. Create your event using one of the methods described earlier.

2. Tap the **Repeat** field.

3. Tap one of the available time intervals: Every day, weekly, every 2 weeks, monthly, or yearly.

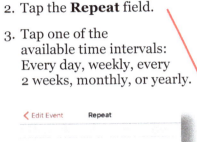

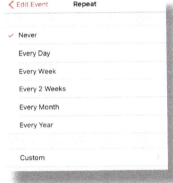

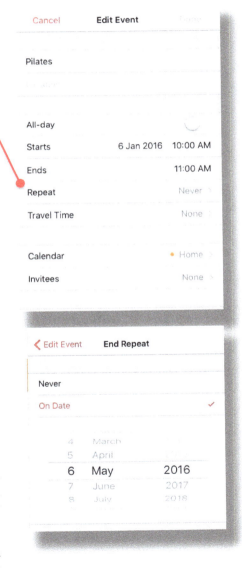

4. You can then specify a date on which your repeating event will end.

5. Choose **End Repeat** to nominate this date.

If you later change an individual event that was created as a repeating event, you will be asked if you wish to change just that particular event, or if you want to apply the change to every future event in the 'repeat' series.

The same applies if you delete an individual event that is part of a 'repeat'.

Adding events from an email, text or Safari

Sometimes, an email, message or Safari page contains date and time information that is highlighted in blue and underlined.

This means that the underlined text is special – if you touch on it, you will link to another App on your device: in this case, to your Calendar.

1. Touch on the Date/time shown in the email/message/web page

2. Select **Create Event**

3. A new event will be created for you, ready for you to finish filling in the details. The title for the event will usually be taken from the email's 'Subject'.

4. Just press **Done** to create the event in your calendar! Easy!

Don't forget those birthdays!

You may or may not have noticed that there is a special 'calendar' that Apple provides for you – one that shows you birthdays and anniversaries.

Birthday and anniversary information can magically appear in your Calendar based on information you have stored about your friends and family in **Contacts**.

Birthday events have a little 'gift box' on their left, and are shown as 'all-day' events (which are at the top of each day).

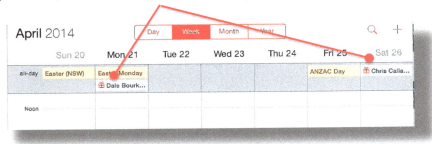

For important people in your life, it is a good idea to add their birthdays to the Contact card you have created for them.

1. Touch on the **Contacts** app on your Home screen.

2. You will find the **Birthday** field immediately after the 'Address' field.

3. Just touch on that field and select the person's birthday – you don't have to choose a year if you don't want to.

Don't forget those birthdays!

But I don't see any birthdays in my Calendar!

If you have set up some birthdays in your **Contacts**, but still don't see these birthdays in your Calendar, it is probably because your 'Birthdays' calendar is not enabled.

We'll cover the concept of 'multiple calendars' a bit later, but for now let's just look at how to make sure you see your **Birthdays** calendar.

1. Touch on **Calendars** at the bottom of the Calendar app's

2. You will see a list of one or more calendars, including a special one in the **Other** category called **Birthdays**.

3. If the **Birthdays** calendar doesn't have a 'tick', then your Contacts' birthdays won't be showing in the calendar.

4. Just touch on the **Birthdays** calendar so that it has a 'tick' on the left hand side.

5. You will also see some other calendars that Apple has provided you with – make sure **Australian Holidays** is ticked if you want to see public holidays in your calendar.

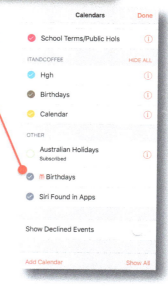

Invite others

Sometimes, an event involves other people in your family, or your friends or colleagues.

When you create an event, you can choose to invite one or more other people to your event. If you do this, those people will receive a notification of the invitation and be able to put your event into their own calendar.

Sending an invitation

Let's look at how you go about inviting others to an event.

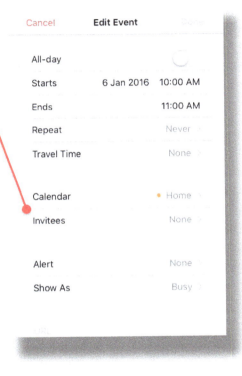

1. When adding or editing your event, touch on the **Invitees** field.

2. As with email, start typing the name of a contact and you will see a list of your Contacts from which to choose – or choose the **+** at top right to select from your list of Contacts

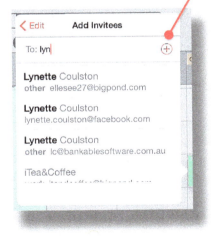

3. If the person is not in your Contacts, type in the email address.

4. Hit return at the end of each email address you enter to show you have finished its entry.

5. Select **< Edit** when all invitees have been nominated.

6. Select **Done** to save the Calendar event and cause notifications to be sent to the invitees about the event.

Invite others

How do I know when I have an invitation?

So, what if someone invites you to an event – how do you receive notification of this invitation?

For one thing, you may notice a number appears on your Calendar App on your Home Screen.

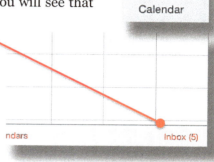

When you go into your Calendar App, you will see that you have the word **Inbox** at the bottom right, showing the same number in brackets.

Touch on this to see you list of invitations.

You can choose to accept, tentatively accept or decline the invitation – the sender of the invitation will then be notified of your action.

Before you accept the invitation, it will appear in your calendar but be 'greyed' to show it is not yet accepted.

Finding events in your Calendar

There are times when you need to search your calendar for an event or appointment.

For example, you may need to answer questions like,

- When did I schedule that next haircut?
- When did I last go to the dentist?
- What date are the parent/teacher interviews?

To perform a search:

1. Touch on the 'Search' symbol

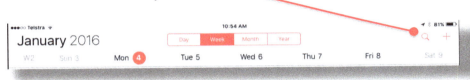

2. Start typing the name of the event you are looking for.
3. You will see a list of events that match what you type.
4. Touch on any event in the returned list to view the details of that event.

My calendar is missing past events

If you find that you are not seeing all past events when you perform a search, it may be that your Calendar is only sync'ing some of your events to your device.

To remedy this (if you have sufficient space on your device to store more of your calendar events), visit **Settings -> Calendar –> Sync.**

From here, you can choose to sync events from last 2 weeks, 1 month, 3 months, 6 months; or choose to sync **All Events.**

Multiple Calendars

You can set up different 'calendars' for events of different types – for example **Home** and **Work** – so that events in these 'calendars' appear as different colours. You can then decide to hide or show individual calendars, and even share your calendar with someone else.

To view your existing set of Calendars

1. Tap Calendars at the bottom of the screen to see the **Show Calendars** screen.

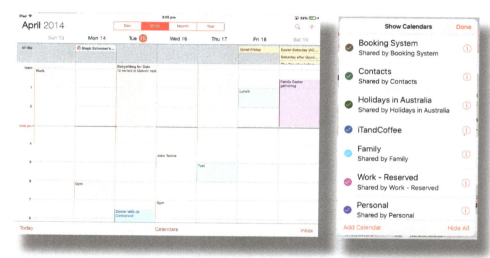

2. You will see a list of Calendars that are already available for you to use on your device.

3. Touch on the ⓘ next to any of the calendars to view or change the name of the calendar, or to change its colour.

4. Change the calendar's colour by touching on a different colour in the list – the current colour will have a tick next to it

   (In the example on the right, the calendar named **Work** is currently purple.)

5. You will also notice the option at the bottom to **Delete Calendar.** Use this to get rid of unwanted calendars.

Multiple Calendars

6. The name of the calendar is shown at the top, and can be changed by touching on the field and removing the existing name with the 'backspace key' and key in a new name.

7. Select **Done** to complete the changes (or **Cancel** if you don't want to make any changes) to return to the list of calendars.

8. On the list of calendar names, tick or untick each calendar to include it in, or exclude it from, your main calendar view.

9. If you want to tell your Calendar App to show all calendars on the Calendar views, touch on 'Show All Calendars' at the top of the list. (This will say 'Hide all Calendars' if you already have selected to show all calendars.)

If ever you find that you are missing some events from your Calendar, make sure to check that a calendar has not become 'unticked'.

Adding a new calendar

You may wish to create a new calendar for certain types of events.

1. Select **Add Calendar** at the bottom left of the **Show Calendars** screen (assuming you have already selected 'Calendars' from the bottom of the screen).

2. Give your calendar a name and choose a colour.

3. Select **Done** – your new Calendar will appear in the list.

4. Ensure that your new Calendar is 'ticked' if you want to see it.

5. Tap **Done** to return to your calendar view, or just tap away from the **Show Calendars** pop-up.

38

Multiple Calendars

To specify the calendar to which an event belongs:

When you add an event (or when you are changing the event after its creation), you can choose the 'calendar' into which it should be placed.

1. When you are creating the event, touch on '>' next to the **Calendar** field.

2. Touch on the applicable calendar to 'tick' it.

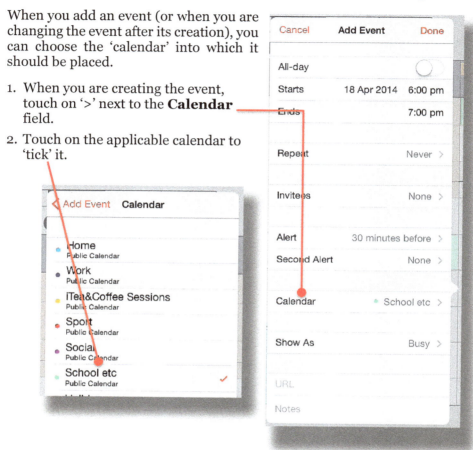

3. The event will now reflect that calendar's colour.

To nominate which calendar is the 'Default' calendar

When you create a new event, a particular Calendar will be the 'default' calendar into which the event is placed.

If you have multiple calendars, you can define which is calendar is to be this default calendar in **Settings -> Calendar -> Default Calendar**

Default Calendar section, tap to choose which calendar should be the default.

Calendar Sharing

Share an iCloud calendar

It can be useful to set up a calendar that is shared with someone else – for example, with another family member or a colleague.

You can share an iCloud calendar with other **iCloud** users. (**Important Note**: The other user must have an iCloud account for this sharing to work.)

When you share a calendar, the person with who you share that calendar can view it, and you can let them add or change events if you like.

You can also share a read-only version that anyone can view, but that can't be updated.

1. In the Show Calendars screen, tap on the ⓘ next to the calendar that you want to share.

2. Touch on the **Add Person**, then choose the person (or people) with whom you want to share the calendar.

3. When finished, touch on **Add**

4. The person will receive an email invitation to join the calendar. They need an Apple ID and iCloud account in order to accept.

5. They will also receive an invitation in the **Inbox** of their calendar.

Turn on/off notifications for shared calendars:

If you have a shared calendar in your list, you may end up receiving lots of notifications about additions, deletions and changes to that shared calendar. You may decide you want to 'turn off' all these notifications. To do this ...

1. Go to **Settings > Notifications > Calendar**.

2. You will see an option for **Shared Calendar Changes**.

3. Turn Off some or all of the **Alerts** options, as well as the **Sounds** and **Badget App Icon**.

Calendar Sharing

To change a person's access to a shared calendar:

1. Tap Calendars, tap Edit, tap the ⓘ next to the shared calendar, then tap the name of a person have shared the calendar with.

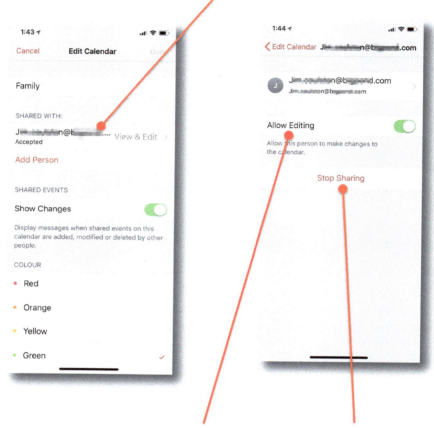

2. You can turn off their ability to edit the calendar or **Stop Sharing** with that person. (Turning off **Allow Editing** means that the person can only view the calendar, but not add or change anything in it.)

3. If you have sent a 'Share' invitation that has not yet been accepted, you will see the option to **Resend** the invitation to join the calendar.

Calendar Sharing

To share a read-only calendar with anyone:

If you want to share your calendar with someone who doesn't have iCloud, it is possible to share a 'read only' version of the calendar as something called a 'Public Calendar'.

1. Tap Calendars, tap Edit, then tap the ⓘ next to the iCloud calendar that you want to share.

2. Turn on **Public Calendar**, then tap **Share Link** to copy or send the URL for the calendar.

3. Anyone can use the URL to subscribe to your calendar using a compatible app, such as Calendar for iOS or OS X.

4. Paste that URL into an email or text to send to the person with whom you want to share.

Subscribing to other non-iCloud Calendars

You can subscribe to other iCloud, Google, Yahoo!, or iCalendar calendars.

You can read events from a *subscribed* calendar on iPad, but you can't edit events or create new ones.

To do this ...

1. Go to **Settings > Accounts & Passwords**

2. Select **Add Account**

3. Select **Other**

4. In the Calendars section and select **Add Subscribed Calendar**

5. Paste in or type in the URL for the subscribed calendar. (Any calendars you subscribe to must use the iCalendar **.ics** format.)

To add something called a **CalDAV** account (for which you *CAN* add to, edit and delete):

1. Follow steps 1-3 as listed in previous walkthrough

2. Under Calendars, tap 'Add CalDAV Account'.

3. You will need to know the configuration details of the Caldav account – fill these in.

Other Calendar Settings

There are several settings in **Settings >Calendar** that affect Calendar and your calendar accounts. Some of these are mentioned in above sections of this guide.

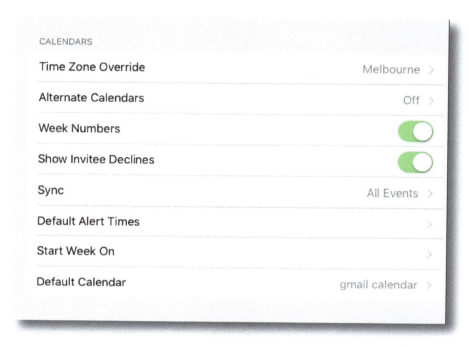

Some others that we have not mentioned earlier are:

- **Time Zone Override** - Calendar time zone, to show dates and times using a different time zone. This is handy if you travel and want to use your home time zone still for your calendar events. Otherwise, I normally leave this setting off.

- **Start Week On** - What day of the week you want your calendar view to show as the first day of the week.

- **Location Suggestions** - If this is 'on', when you type the location of an event, suggested locations will be shown for you to choose from.

- **Siri & Search** - which controls whether information from 'Calendar can appear in 'Search and Look Up'. It also allows you to included suggested events in you calendar – for example, if an event is found in a mail message or text.

Other Guides in the **Introduction to the iPad and iPhone** Series

* **A Guided Tour of the iPad and iPhone**
* **Taking Photos and Videos**
* **Viewing and Managing Photos and Videos**
* **Typing and Editing**
* **Keeping in Touch: The Mail App**
* **Keeping in Touch: The Phone App**
* **Exploring the Internet on Safari**
* **Let's Go Shopping – Exploring the Stores**
* **Discovering iBooks**
* **Getting Connected**